STEM IN

SNOWBOARDING

SportsZone

An Imprint of Abdo Publishing
abdopublishing.com

BY DONNA B. MCKINNEY

ABDOPUBLISHING.COM

Published by Abdo Publishing, a division of ABDO, PO Box 398166, Minneapolis, Minnesota 55439.
Copyright © 2018 by Abdo Consulting Group, Inc. International copyrights reserved in all countries.
No part of this book may be reproduced in any form without written permission from the
publisher. SportsZone™ is a trademark and logo of Abdo Publishing.

Printed in the United States of America, North Mankato, Minnesota
102017
012018

Cover Photo: Dmytro Vietrov/Shutterstock Images
Interior Photos: Dmytro Vietrov/Shutterstock Images, 1, 12–13; Dmitry Molchanov/Shutterstock
Images, 4–5; Jerry Cleveland/The Denver Post/Getty Images, 7; Shutterstock Images, 8, 14–15, 17,
40; Mikkel William/iStockphoto, 10; iStockphoto, 19 (left), 19 (middle), 19 (right); Nathan Bilow/AP
Images, 20–21; Javier Soriano/AFP/Getty Images, 23; Konstantin Shishkin/Shutterstock Images,
25 (bottom); Golden Sikorka/Shutterstock Images, 25 (top); Ilmars Znotins/AFP/Getty Images, 27;
Sergey Furtaev/Shutterstock Images, 28–29; Elaine Thompson/AP Images, 31; Barracuda Designs/
Shutterstock Images, 32–33; Kelvin Degree/Shutterstock Images, 34; Ventura/Shutterstock Images,
36–37; Mikhail Metzel/AP Images, 39; Sergei Grits/AP Images, 42; Dennis van de Water/Shutterstock
Images, 44–45

Editor: Arnold Ringstad
Series Designer: Maggie Villaume
Content Consultant: Mark Denny, PhD, author, *Gliding for Gold: The Physics of Winter Sports*

PUBLISHER'S CATALOGING-IN-PUBLICATION DATA

Names: McKinney, Donna B., author.
Title: STEM in snowboarding / by Donna B. McKinney.
Description: Minneapolis, Minnesota : Abdo Publishing, 2018. | Series: STEM in sports | Includes
        online resources and index.
Identifiers: LCCN 2017946887 | ISBN 9781532113529 (lib.bdg.) | ISBN 9781532152405 (ebook)
Subjects: LCSH: Snowboarding--Juvenile literature. | Sports sciences--Juvenile literature. | Physics-
        -Juvenile literature.
Classification: DDC 796.939--dc23
LC record available at https://lccn.loc.gov/2017946887

TABLE OF CONTENTS

Along with a rider's skills, STEM principles help make thrilling snowboarding runs possible.

CHAPTER 1

STEM ON THE SLOPES

The snowboarders glide down the snowy mountain. As they carve new paths in the powder, they are actually sliding over a thin film of water. The friction of their boards melts the snow, creating this water. The boards have been skillfully engineered to withstand stresses and cold temperatures. The snowboarders shift their positions as they ride. Maintaining their balance takes practice and skill. They make tiny adjustments to keep their center of gravity over the board. The snowboarders reach a jump, and one after another they go airborne. As soon as they leave the ramp, gravity begins pulling them back to Earth. While spinning in the air, they travel in a smooth arc back down to the slope. A tiny camera strapped to one of the snowboarders' helmets captures all the action.

Snowboarding can be fun and exciting. Some snowboarders zoom down mountainsides, slicing through the snow. Others catch huge air on jumps, pulling off impressive tricks. Underlying all of these thrills are principles of STEM (science, technology, engineering, and math).

FROM SNURFING TO SNOWBOARDING

An engineer named Sherman Poppen invented snowboarding in the 1960s. His first snowboard was just two skis fastened together. There was a rope on one end to help the rider steer. Poppen's wife, Nancy, called this first board a "snurfer" because it seemed like a mixture of snow and surfing. Poppen is known

Snowboarding became more widespread and popular in the 1980s.

as the "grandfather of snowboarding." The sport gained popularity over the next few decades. In 1998 snowboarding was an Olympic sport for the first time.

People who want to snowboard need to have the right gear. At the top of the list are the three Bs: the

Protective gear helps keep riders safe, warm, and comfortable.

boots, board, and bindings. The bindings clip the rider's
boots to the board. Safety gear is also important. Riders
can move very fast, and jumps can take them high in
the air. A fall could be dangerous. A helmet protects the
boarder's head when falls happen. A jacket and snow
pants keep the boarder warm and dry.

At first, snowboarders usually focus on simply holding their balance on the board. As they gain skills, they may focus on some different kinds of snowboarding. Some boarders like to race down mountainsides. Other boarders enjoy doing tricks, jumping and spinning on their boards. In the Winter Olympics, snowboarders compete in both race and trick events.

THE STEM OF SNOWBOARDING

Science helps explain the things that happen when a person rides a snowboard. How are riders able to balance, and why do they sometimes fall? Concepts such as gravity, friction, and momentum explain how snowboards move.

Technology has made the sport of snowboarding safer and more exciting than ever. Fog-free goggles give snowboarders a clearer view. Helmets protect boarders' heads. Communication gear in the helmets helps them talk to each other. Wearable devices tell them where

Helmet-mounted cameras allow snowboarders to do hands-free recording of their runs.

they are and how active they've been. High-tech cameras record all the action. Gloves keep boarders warm and let them wirelessly control phones or cameras. Today's technology protects and equips snowboarders in ways only dreamed of in the past.

Engineers design snowboards in a variety of sizes, shapes, and materials. They decide how flexible a board should be. All these factors influence how a snowboard will move and handle. Different types of board are better suited for particular styles of snowboarding. Long before a snowboarder hits the slopes, engineers have already put work into crafting the perfect board.

There's math in the world of snowboarding too. Math shows up in the board design. Boarders describe their tricks by naming the number of degrees of rotation they go through. Angles are used to tell how steep a mountain is. Much of the action in snowboarding can be described in terms of math.

STEM is a part of snowboarding in so many ways. Along with the added fun, STEM brings more safety to the sport too. Today the sport can be a thrilling activity for everyone from beginners to experts. Even if a snowboarder is not thinking about STEM while racing down a mountain or pulling off a cool trick, these principles are still at work.

Gravity's downhill pull gives snowboarders the speed to pull off jumps and tricks.

CHAPTER

2

SNOWBOARDING SCIENCE

Gravity is the force that pulls objects with mass toward each other. Large objects have much stronger gravity than small ones. Earth's gravity is powerful. It pulls everything on or near the planet, including people, toward the planet's center. Without gravity, snowboarding wouldn't be possible. Gravity's downward pull is what gives snowboarders speed as they travel downhill. Unlike with a skateboard, snowboarders can't take one foot off the

board to push themselves forward. They rely on gravity to provide all of their forward motion.

On Earth's surface, an object's center of gravity is an imaginary point located at the average position of its

mass. If the object were to be supported at this point, it would remain perfectly balanced. For a person, this location is usually in the middle of the body, about an inch above the navel. Boarders must keep their center of gravity over the board to keep their balance when not accelerating. If their center of gravity goes beyond the board, there is a higher chance they will fall.

USING FRICTION

Friction is a force that acts when two objects come in contact with each other. It slows the objects down, and the energy of motion that is lost is turned into heat. When a snowboard slides over snow, friction melts a thin layer of the snow, creating a film of water that the snowboard glides across. Snowboarders actually ride the board down the mountain atop this thin film of water.

The pull of gravity gives snowboarders speed as they go down a slope. Going fast can be fun. But going

WET AND DRY SNOW

Not all snow is the same. Depending on the air temperature, snow can be "wet" or "dry." Slushy, wet snow occurs when the temperature is just above freezing. Powdery, dry, fluffy snow results from colder temperatures. For snowboarders, colder temperatures usually produce the best snow. Thick powder is easiest to snowboard in, and it can cushion a boarder's falls.

too fast can cause a boarder to lose control. So snowboarders move in a zig-zag pattern, cutting back and forth down the mountain. These zig-zag moves create extra friction. That friction slows them down. By slowing their speed, boarders can control their paths more easily.

FORCES AND MOTION IN THE HALF-PIPE

Not all snowboarders ride down mountainsides. Some boarders like the thrill of the half-pipe. In this long, U-shaped downhill ramp, boarders perform jumps and tricks. Gravity, speed, and balance are at work in the half-pipe. The forces involved are slightly different from those on a mountain slope.

In a half-pipe, boarders first gain speed. Then they turn hard to zoom up one of the pipe's sides. They leave the lip of the half-pipe and go soaring into the air. They perform a trick or spin. As gravity pulls them back down, their speed decreases to zero. Gravity then accelerates them as they return to the half-pipe. They land, then glide over to the other side of the half-pipe to repeat the process.

POTENTIAL ENERGY

POTENTIAL ENERGY

POTENTIAL ENERGY

KINETIC ENERGY

KINETIC ENERGY

KINETIC ENERGY

Kinetic energy is the energy of motion. Potential energy is the energy an object has due to its position. An object in the air has potential energy because gravity is acting on it and will pull it downward. Snowboarders in half-pipes are repeatedly trading kinetic energy and potential energy. As boarders ride up the side of the half-pipe, most of their energy is kinetic energy. They are moving at top speed. When they fly into the air, they slow down. At their highest point, their speed reaches zero. All of their kinetic energy has been replaced by potential energy. As gravity pulls them back down, that potential energy is traded for kinetic energy. The process repeats with each jump.

Advanced goggles protect snowboarders from the sun's blinding glare.

3

HIGH-TECH GEAR

Technology has taken giant steps forward since the first snowboard hit the slopes in the 1960s. Today's snowboarders have gear that had not been dreamed of a few decades ago. Modern technology helps make snowboarding safer and more fun.

GOGGLES THAT CLEAR THE FOG

Basic goggles are important gear for boarders. They protect the eyes in a fall. They also block wind, flying snow, and glare from the sun. Today's high-tech goggles do all that and more. The most advanced ones come with sensors that tell the boarder's speed, distance traveled, and altitude.

Fogging is a common problem with goggles. The chilly outdoor air cools the lens. At the same time, air from the boarder's body warms the lens. Where the warm air and cold lens meet, tiny water drops form on the inside of the lens. The lens fogs over, blocking the snowboarder's view. Boarders need to see well all the time, so fogging can be a big problem.

Antifog goggles provide a solution. Some goggles come with vents and small fans to prevent fogging. Other goggles have a thin film on the lens that heats up. It works somewhat like the defroster on a car's rear window. The snowboarder pushes a button on the goggles, the film warms, and the fog goes away.

SMART HELMETS

Helmets help prevent head injuries in a fall. Swedish researchers came up with a technology called a

Helmets absorb the blows of hard falls, protecting a rider's head.

multidirectional impact protection system (MIPS). MIPS
is used in both snow helmets and bike helmets. The
helmets have two layers that can rotate independently
of each other. This reduces the impact of a sudden hit to

the head, lowering the chance of a brain injury when a boarder crashes. Many helmet brands are made with the MIPS system.

In addition to safety, some helmet technologies are for enjoyment or convenience. Headphones are built into some helmets, letting boarders listen to music as they ride. Others include microphones, letting the rider answer a phone call while gliding down the slopes.

WATCHES THAT TELL MORE THAN TIME

Snowboarders can use sophisticated devices on their wrists to get valuable data as they ride. Many of today's devices feature global positioning system (GPS) technology. They can communicate with GPS satellites in orbit around Earth to determine the rider's exact location. The boarder can figure out how far down the mountain he or she is.

Thanks to the location information from GPS, these wearable devices can also measure a rider's speed and total distance traveled. A wireless data connection can

The global positioning system is useful for snowboarders. It can help them navigate mountains they've never been to before. It also lets them record a new route down a favorite slope. If they get lost in a remote area, GPS can help them find their way to safety.

Multiple GPS satellites send out signals. A GPS watch receives these signals. Part of the signal includes exactly when the signal was sent. By comparing this time with the time the signal was received, the watch can tell exactly how far away it is from the satellite that sent the signal. When it receives multiple signals, it can tell how far it is from each satellite. This allows the GPS watch to determine its location.

receive weather alerts and pass them along to the rider. If a blizzard is coming on, the rider can seek shelter.

CAMERAS THAT RECORD THE RIDE

An ordinary camera likely would not last long in the tough conditions of snowboarding. Snowboarders use action cameras instead. These are small, rugged digital cameras made to take a beating. A boarder can wear an action camera mounted on the helmet or strapped to some other part of the body. These cameras record what the snowboarder sees riding down the mountain or performing a trick. Some of the cameras are controlled by voice. The user can tell the camera to start or pause

DRONEBOARDING

Drones are small flying machines that usually have four or more downward-facing rotors. They are controlled remotely. Drones have become popular in recent years. So maybe it's no surprise that someone dreamed up the idea of droneboarding. A pilot controls a powerful drone. That powerful drone tows a snowboarder through the snow.

Advancing technology has enabled the new sport of droneboarding.

a recording. Today's models have sharp, detailed video quality. With a camera, a boarder can share the thrill of the ride with others.

GLOVES WITH FINGER-TIP TECHNOLOGY

Thanks to technology, a snowboarder's gloves do much more than just keep hands warm. Snow gloves can have wireless communication built in. This means boarders do not need to take off gloves to control their music or make a phone call. The wearer controls the phone and the music just by touching specific fingers together.

Different snowboards are better suited for different types of snow and snowboarding events.

CHAPTER

4

ENGINEERING A RUN

Snowboards consist of layers of different materials. These materials are chosen to create sturdy boards. Examining these layers helps reveal the engineering that makes snowboarding possible.

THE CORE

Most boards are made with wood at the core. Common wood choices are poplar, aspen, ash, and birch. Bamboo has come into use more recently. These woods are used because they vibrate less than other kinds. In a process called laminating, the wood is first cut into long strips. Then these strips are glued together, and the wood is cut to the shape of the board. Engineers arrange the wood layers in different patterns. They can also vary the woods used. This gives boards different strengths and weights.

FIBERGLASS LAYERS

After the core is complete, fiberglass layers are added. Fiberglass makes the board stiff. It helps the board keep its shape through the wear and tear of snowboarding. The fiberglass can wrap the core in different ways. By changing the wraps, the board is either more stiff or more flexible. A sticky material called resin is applied in these fiberglass layers to protect and bind them.

BINDINGS

Snowboard bindings connect the boarder's boots to the board. Most bindings are made of urethane (which is like plastic but stronger), carbon, or an aluminum alloy. Today's bindings are strong, yet lightweight. There is a wide variety in binding materials and the ways they are made.

Snowboarders choose boards and other gear that match their style and skills.

TOPSHEET

The topsheet is the part of the board that can be seen. Different materials are used for the topsheet. These include nylon, wood, fiberglass, and composites. The topsheet protects the inner layers of the board. It also

On tight turns, snowboarders touch the ground as their boards tilt sharply.

gives the rider a place to express himself or herself with colorful graphics.

BASE

The base is the board's bottom. It's the part that touches the snow. Board bases are made from plastic. The base

ROCKER

REGULAR CAMBER

MIXED CAMBER

FLAT

KEY

AREA OF
CONTACT
WITH SNOW

BOARD PROFILES

The term *camber* describes the arched or curved shape of the board. For many years, most boards were regular camber. This means they touch the snow only near the board's tip and tail. This results in a stable ride. In recent years, other camber options have appeared. The rocker style touches the snow only in the middle between the bindings. In the flat style, everything but the tip and tail rests flat on the snow. It allows faster turns. The mixed camber option combines the regular camber and rocker board. Each profile design has its pros and cons. Thanks to the progress in board design, snowboarders have many choices.

is made in one of two ways: extrusion or sintering. In extrusion, the base is made from a thin sheet of melted plastic. Extruded boards cost less than sintered boards. They are easy to repair. The ride on an extruded base is slower than on a sintered one. In sintering, plastic is made into a powder, heated, and pressed. Sintered boards absorb wax well, and they provide a faster ride than extruded boards. Sintered boards are sturdier, but they also cost more than extruded ones. They are harder to repair, too.

SIDEWALLS AND EDGES

A snowboard's sidewall is the area around its outer edge. It is usually made of plastic. Rubber layers are added too. The rubber helps ease the bumps of snowboarding. The outermost edge of the board is made of metal. It cuts easily through the ice and snow.

Snowboarders often have to consider the math of
rotations and timing when pulling off big tricks.

5

SNOWBOARDING AND MATH

Just like science, technology, and engineering, math plays important roles in snowboarding. Numbers are used to talk about topics from mountains to spins to boards.

MATH OF BOARD DESIGN

The language of math is used in snowboard design. The curve of the board's edges can vary. This curve is called the sidecut radius. The sidecut radius tells how narrow the board is in the middle. The deeper sidecut

boards are more narrow. This narrow-in-the-middle design is usually good for snowboarders who are just beginning. The shallow sidecut boards are wider in the middle. This wider design is usually good for boarders who ride at higher speeds. It's also a good board for riding in powdery snow with lumpy, slippery patches.

SPINNING DOWN THE MOUNTAIN

Angles are measured in degrees. There are 360 degrees in a circle. This makes up one complete revolution. Snowboarders use numbers of degrees to describe their spins. A boarder might perform a 360-degree spin on the snow or in the air. Beginning boarders make a half spin, turning through 180 degrees. As their skill grows, they jump higher in the air. The extra time in the air gives them more time to spin. They may make one and a half complete revolutions (540 degrees) or even two (720 degrees).

In 2015, British snowboarder Billy Morgan successfully landed an 1800 at a resort in Italy. He flew into the air

The huge half-pipe structures used for competitions give snowboarders a chance to fly high into the air on each jump.

180°   **360°**   **1800°**

Spins are often combined with grabbing the board and doing other body movements in midair to make up complex snowboarding tricks. To start a spin, a snowboarder first needs to build up speed and jump off a ramp or hill. While building up speed, the boarder winds his or her arms or body in the opposite direction of the planned spin. When he or she goes into the air, the arms are thrown in the direction of the spin to begin the motion. Before landing, the spinning motion must be slowed down so that the boarder can come down smoothly.

off a huge ramp and rotated through five complete revolutions before landing. The spin was combined with grabbing the board and going through several flips, resulting in a trick known as a backside 1800 quadruple cork. After the incredible feat, Morgan said, "I've been thinking about this for so long, it's such a relief to have it done. It could have been cleaner, but I'm still pumped."

WHAT SIZE SNOWBOARD?

In the early days of snowboarding, there was a simple way to tell which size snowboard was right for a particular rider. The person simply set the snowboard on end. If the tip of the board reached the person's chin, then it was the right size. Today's snowboard sizing takes both height and weight into account.

The type of snowboarding a person plans on doing should also factor into choosing a snowboard size. Riding down a mountainside is easier with a longer board, which provides stability and speed. Riding in a half-pipe is easier with a shorter board, which is more maneuverable and spins better.

MATH IN ACTION

Billy Morgan has amazed the snowboarding world with his stunning spins and flips.

NUMBERS TELL THE TALE OF THE MOUNTAIN

Math can help a snowboarder better understand mountains. Most ski resorts publish number facts about their slopes. There are several figures that can help snowboarders plan their runs. They include the elevation, the vertical drop, and the longest run number.

Elevation is the mountain's height at any given point. It is common to see the elevation listed for the mountain top and bottom. Vertical drop is the distance from the top of the snowboarder's route to the bottom. Knowing the vertical drop tells snowboarders how much land they will cover on the ride. The longest run number, as the name suggests, provides the length of the longest ski or snowboarding run. Most boarders prefer long runs, so resorts usually advertise their longest run. These numbers can help boarders learn which resorts and mountains might be best suited to their skill level.

STEM BEHIND SNOWBOARDING

Science, technology, engineering, and math come together to make snowboarding a thrilling, competitive, and safe sport for riders around the world. Whether

snowboarders are enjoying a relaxing weekend on a mountain or riding for an Olympic gold medal, they can use STEM principles on the slopes.

GLOSSARY

CORE
The inside or center of a snowboard.

ELEVATION
The height of a mountain.

FIBERGLASS
A strong, lightweight material made from glass fiber and plastic.

FRICTION
The force that results when two objects rub against each other.

HALF-PIPE
A snow-covered, U-shaped ramp. Boarders use it to perform jumps and other tricks.

KINETIC ENERGY
The energy of motion.

SNURFER
The name of the first snowboard, invented in the 1960s. *Snurfer* combines the words "snow" and "surfer."

TOPSHEET
The part of the snowboard that can be seen. Colorful graphics are applied on the topsheet.

VERTICAL DROP
The distance from the top to the bottom of the mountain.

ONLINE RESOURCES

Booklinks
NONFICTION NETWORK
FREE! ONLINE NONFICTION RESOURCES

To learn more about STEM in snowboarding, visit
abdobooklinks.com. These links are routinely monitored and
updated to provide the most current information available.

MORE INFORMATION

BOOKS

Hamilton, John. *Snowboarding*. Minneapolis, MN: Abdo
Publishing, 2015.

Howell, Brian. *Great Moments in Olympic Snowboarding*.
Minneapolis, MN: Abdo Publishing, 2015.

Schwartz, Heather E. *Snowboarding*. Detroit, MI: Lucent Books,
2011.

INDEX

ABOUT THE AUTHOR

Donna B. McKinney worked for the US Navy for more than 30 years, writing about science and technology topics. Now she writes for children and adults as a full-time freelancer. She holds a bachelor's degree from Campbell University and a master's degree from George Mason University.